Cal and Lucy were
They lived next do
and did many thing together.

1

One day Cal and Lucy were playing out
in back of Cal's house. His mother
came to the back door and
called to them.
"I have some work to do," she said.
"Would you be willing to come in
and look after the baby?"

2

Cal and Lucy were happy to help, as long as it was the two of them together.
Then it would be more like playing than helping.

"I'll be in there," said Cal's mother. "If Billy starts to cry, give him something to eat."

At first the baby was sleeping, so Cal
and Lucy played a game together.
But Billy didn't sleep for long.
And when he saw the children playing,
he started to cry.

"Your mother said to give him something to eat," said Lucy.

So Cal gave Billy something to eat.
But that didn't work.
Billy wouldn't eat.
He just went on crying.

"How can we get him to stop crying?"
asked Lucy.
"I'll give him something to play with,"
said Cal.

So Cal gave Billy something
to play with.
But that didn't work.
Billy wouldn't play.
He just went on crying.

"How can we get him to stop crying?" asked Lucy.

"We can make funny faces," said Cal.

So Cal and Lucy made funny faces.
But that didn't work.
Billy couldn't see the funny faces.
He was crying too much.

"I give up!" said Cal.
"How can we get him to stop
crying?"

"Could we read to him?" asked Lucy.

"I never thought of that," said Cal.

"But we can try and see if it works."

First Lucy read to Billy.
And it worked!
He stopped crying!

Cal read next and it still worked.
Billy didn't cry anymore.

Now when Lucy and Cal look after Billy,
they read to him.
And Cal's mother always says, "You children
can look after Billy anytime you like!"